UP AND AWAY!

Taking a Flight

by MEREDITH DAVIS • Illustrated by KEN DUBROWSKI

An airport is a hive of activity. Airplanes continually land and take off, carrying passengers and cargo all over the world. Workers are everywhere, making sure passengers will have a safe and pleasant trip.

AIR TRAFFIC CONTROL TOWER

RUNWAY

TAXIWAY

EXIT 6 AIRPORT

TERMINAL B

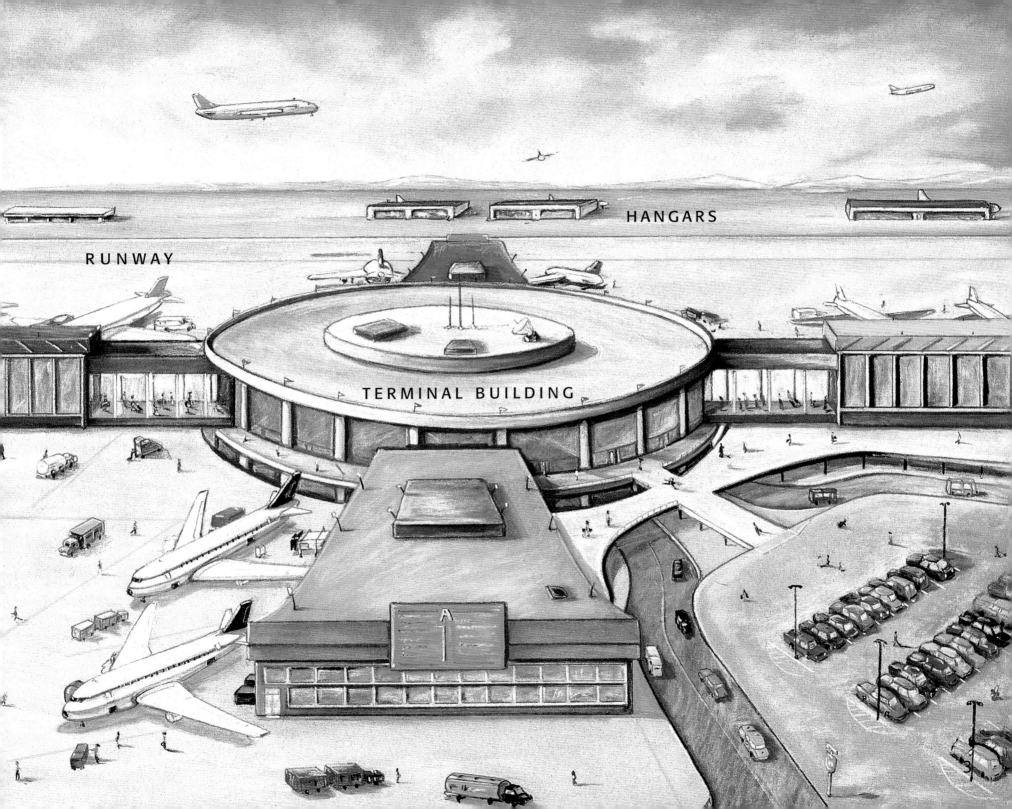

RUNWAY

HANGARS

TERMINAL BUILDING

TERMINAL AND CONCOURSE

When passengers arrive at the airport they enter the terminal building. After checking in, they go to the concourse where they wait to board the plane. Passengers may also visit the terminal's restaurants and shops.

Passengers walk to the concourse. They may also ride escalators, electric subways, or moving sidewalks.

Upon entering the terminal, passengers' baggage may be X-rayed to check for dangerous objects.

Passengers show their tickets and passports and are given boarding passes that show their destination, flight number, and seat number.

Baggage is weighed, labeled, and put on a conveyor belt.

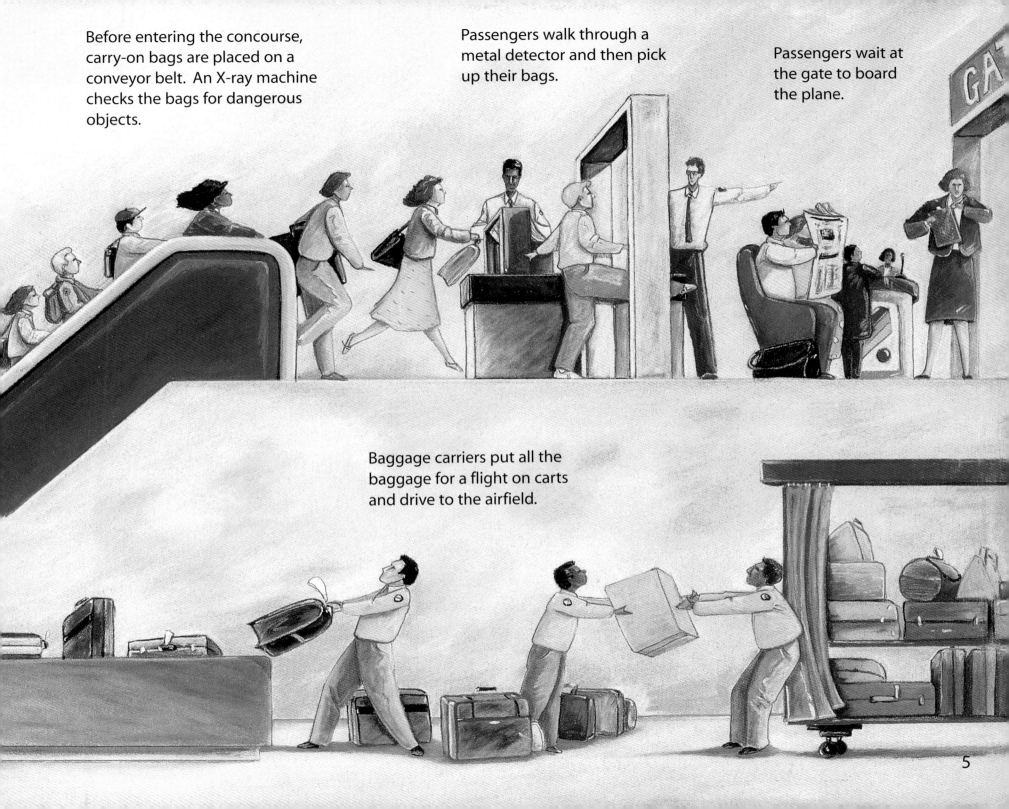

Before entering the concourse, carry-on bags are placed on a conveyor belt. An X-ray machine checks the bags for dangerous objects.

Passengers walk through a metal detector and then pick up their bags.

Passengers wait at the gate to board the plane.

Baggage carriers put all the baggage for a flight on carts and drive to the airfield.

5

CATERING

Before a flight takes off, meals and snacks for passengers and crew are prepared and loaded onto the plane.

1. Every day, fresh ingredients are bought and stored in large refrigerators in airport kitchens. Catering staff prepares meals, snacks, and drinks.

2. Meals are stored in carts and transported to the plane. Dry ice keeps the food cold. The food storage unit of a high lift catering truck rises up to the plane by hydraulic power.

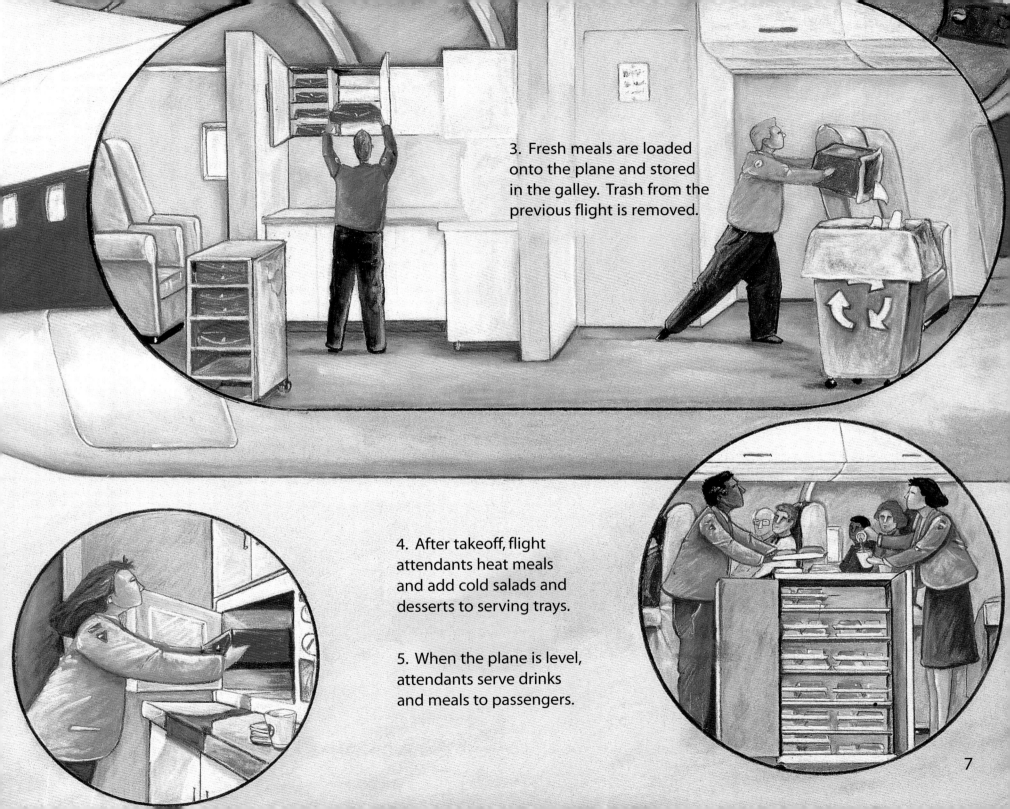

3. Fresh meals are loaded onto the plane and stored in the galley. Trash from the previous flight is removed.

4. After takeoff, flight attendants heat meals and add cold salads and desserts to serving trays.

5. When the plane is level, attendants serve drinks and meals to passengers.

7

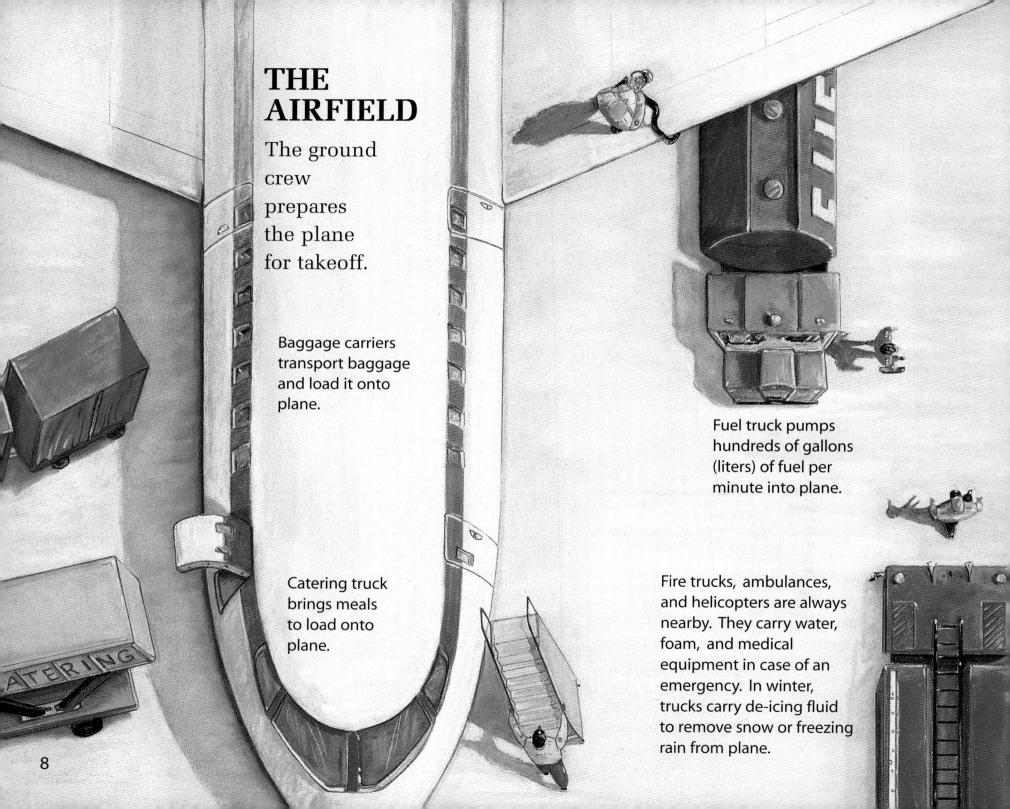

THE AIRFIELD

The ground crew prepares the plane for takeoff.

Baggage carriers transport baggage and load it onto plane.

Catering truck brings meals to load onto plane.

Fuel truck pumps hundreds of gallons (liters) of fuel per minute into plane.

Fire trucks, ambulances, and helicopters are always nearby. They carry water, foam, and medical equipment in case of an emergency. In winter, trucks carry de-icing fluid to remove snow or freezing rain from plane.

8

Wiffy dumper truck pumps out dirty water from toilets and replaces it with fresh water and disinfectant.

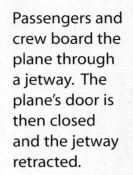

Passengers and crew board the plane through a jetway. The plane's door is then closed and the jetway retracted.

Water truck delivers water to plane or pumps water in from underground tanks.

Trash and unused food from previous flight are removed.

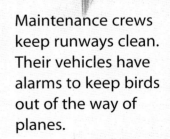

Maintenance crews keep runways clean. Their vehicles have alarms to keep birds out of the way of planes.

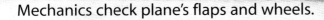

Mechanics check plane's flaps and wheels.

PREPARATIONS ON THE PLANE

The cockpit crew is usually made up of the captain, the pilot (also called the first officer), and the flight engineer. Each crew member has different jobs to complete before takeoff.

Gear lever?

Start switch?

Before boarding, the captain receives the flight plan from the dispatch office. The plan gives the plane's route, altitudes, and the speed needed for take off. The captain also checks the weather forecast and wind speed.

The flight engineer checks the plane's gauges and switches to make sure they are in the right positions for takeoff.

The cockpit can have over 970 different instruments and controls, so the crew members carefully review what they have done. They check a list of more than 100 items before the plane is ready for takeoff.

The pilot programs the plane's computers with the flight plan. Once the plane is airborne, the computers control the plane's speed, altitude, and direction.

In the cabins, passengers find their seats. Flight attendants make sure carry-on bags are stored in overhead compartments or under the seats, and they check the catering equipment and supplies.

11

AIR TRAFFIC CONTROL

Air traffic controllers guide the plane during takeoff, flight, and landing. They use computers, cameras, radar, and radios to keep planes a safe distance from each other on the ground and in the air. Air traffic controllers work fast because the planes they watch are traveling at over 600 miles (965 kilometers) per hour. At the world's busiest airport, in Chicago, a plane takes off or lands every 40 seconds.

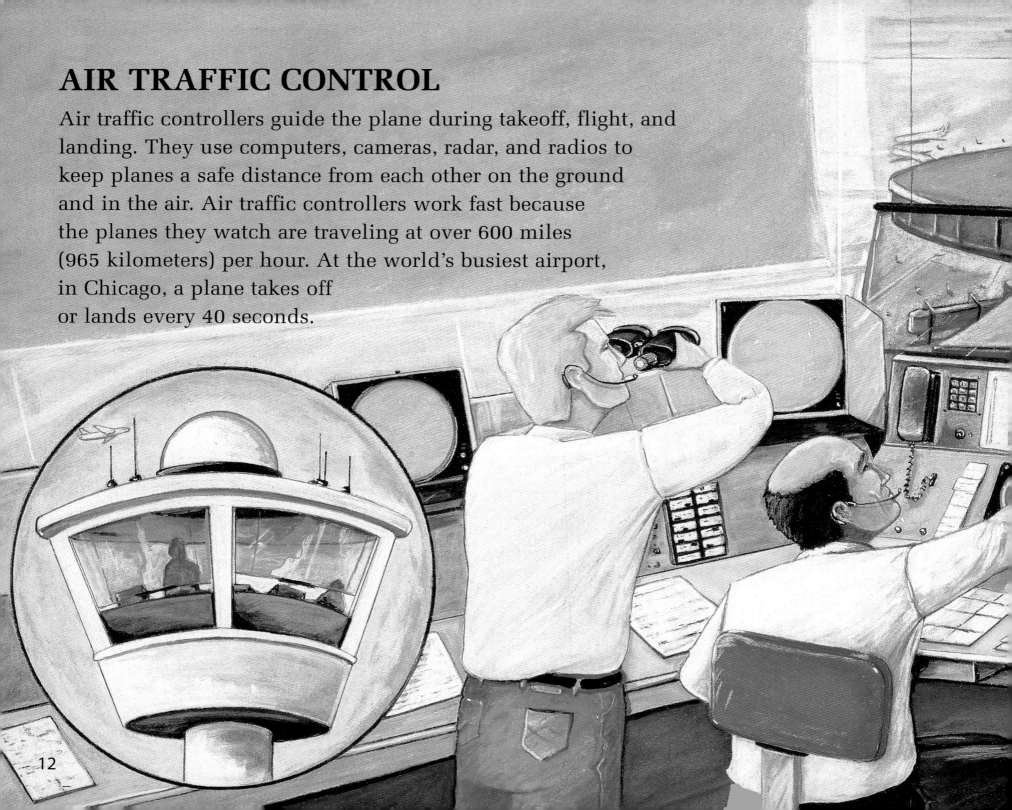

Radar screens show controllers the location, speed, direction, and identity of every plane in the area, even in the dark, rain, or heavy fog.

TAKEOFF

After the plane is loaded and the crew
has finished its preflight checks, the
captain starts the engines and follows
instructions from the control tower
to guide the plane to the taxiway.

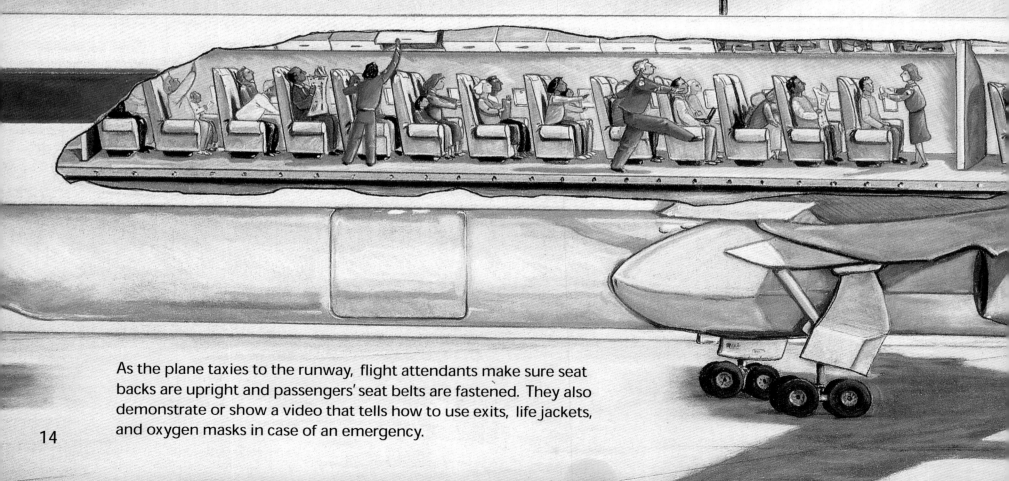

As the plane taxies to the runway, flight attendants make sure seat
backs are upright and passengers' seat belts are fastened. They also
demonstrate or show a video that tells how to use exits, life jackets,
and oxygen masks in case of an emergency.

About 600 feet (185 meters) from the runway, the tower clears the plane for takeoff. The captain sets the flaps, brings the engines to full power, and the plane speeds down the runway. When the air rushing over the wings gives the plane enough lift to leave the ground, the captain raises the nose and the plane takes off. The pilot then retracts the wheels.

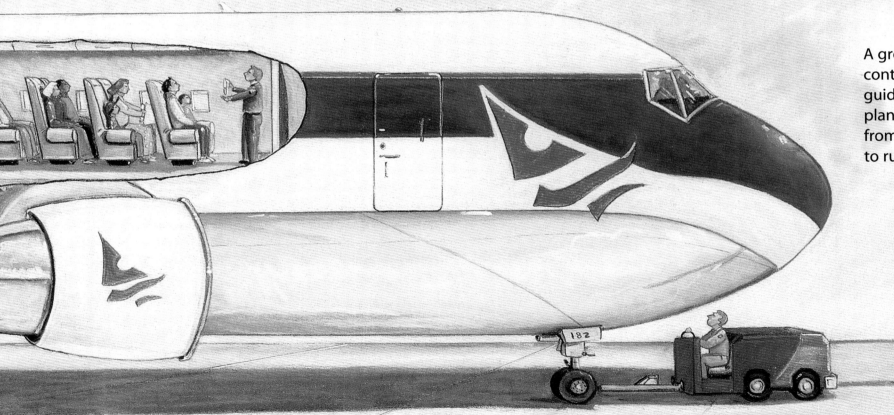

A ground controller guides the plane safely from taxiway to runway.

A pushback tug moves the plane away from gate.

FLIGHT AND LANDING

For most of the flight, a computer flies the plane,
but the crew still carefully monitors the controls.
If air turbulence makes the ride bumpy,
passengers are asked to stay seated and fasten
their seat belts.

Passengers may walk around, talk,
read, work, play, sleep, look out
windows, or enjoy music or a movie.

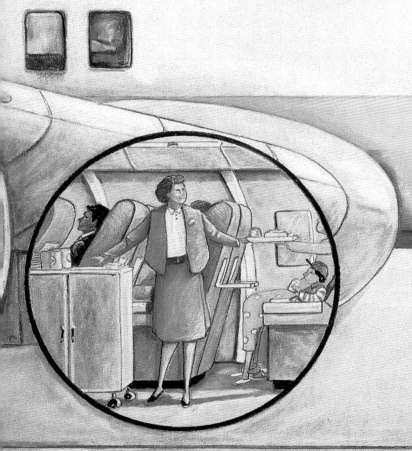

Flight attendants serve food
and drinks.

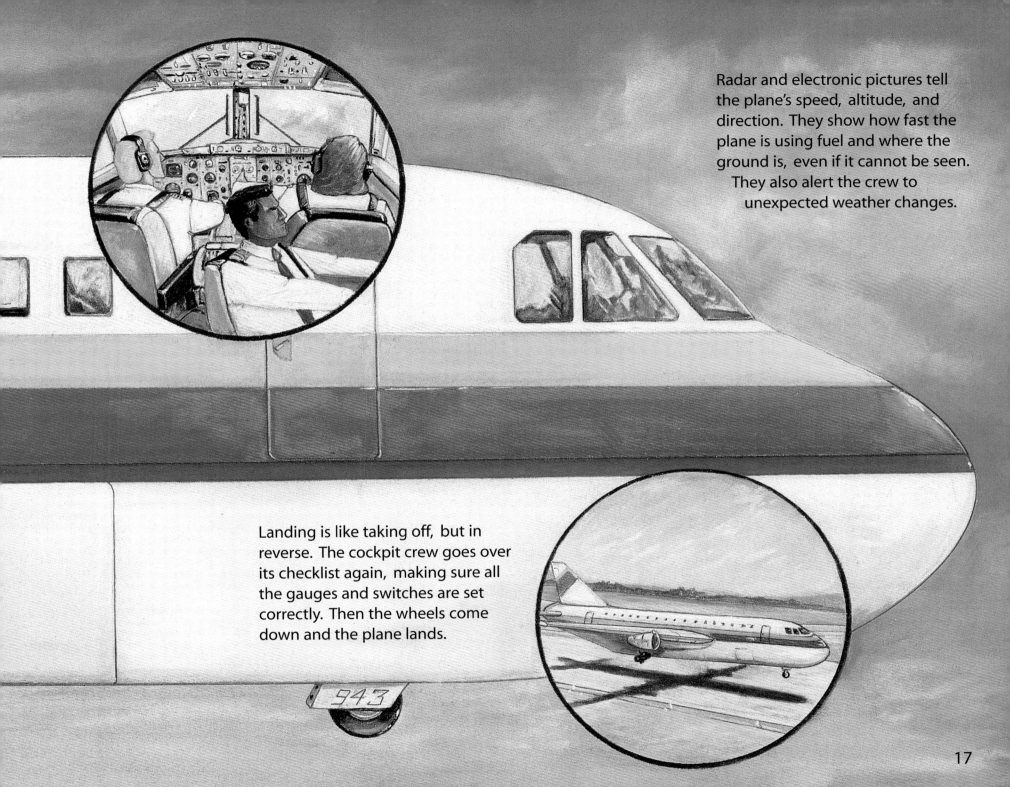

Radar and electronic pictures tell the plane's speed, altitude, and direction. They show how fast the plane is using fuel and where the ground is, even if it cannot be seen. They also alert the crew to unexpected weather changes.

Landing is like taking off, but in reverse. The cockpit crew goes over its checklist again, making sure all the gauges and switches are set correctly. Then the wheels come down and the plane lands.

943

ARRIVAL

When passengers arrive from a foreign country they go through immigration, pick up their baggage, and go through customs.

An immigration officer looks at passengers' passports to see if they are allowed into the country. Sometimes the officer will also stamp passports.

IMMIGRATION

Baggage is taken off the plane and brought to a carousel in the terminal so passengers can collect their bags.

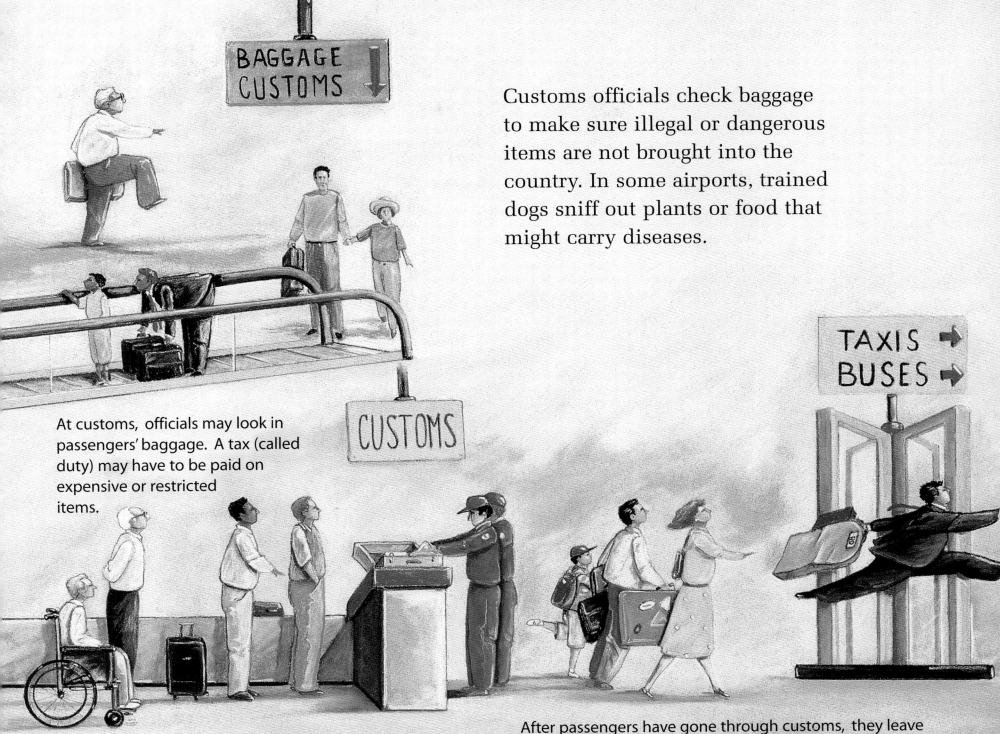

BAGGAGE CUSTOMS ↓

Customs officials check baggage to make sure illegal or dangerous items are not brought into the country. In some airports, trained dogs sniff out plants or food that might carry diseases.

At customs, officials may look in passengers' baggage. A tax (called duty) may have to be paid on expensive or restricted items.

CUSTOMS

TAXIS →
BUSES →

After passengers have gone through customs, they leave the terminal to begin their vacations or business trips. 19

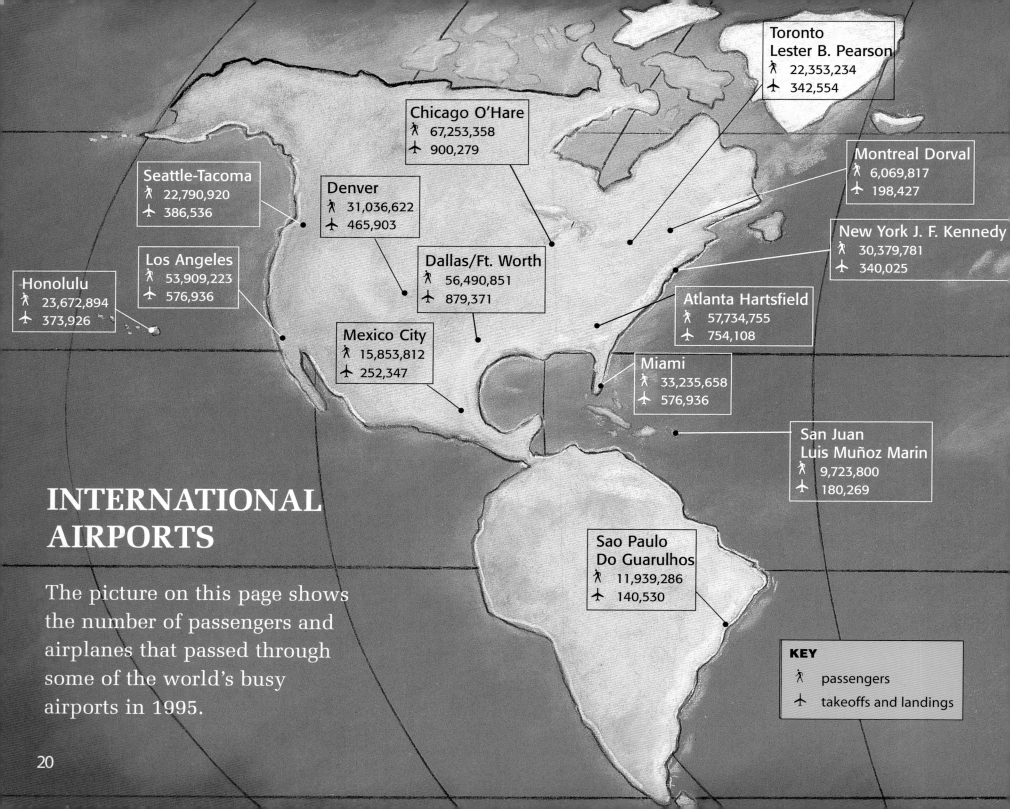

INTERNATIONAL AIRPORTS

The picture on this page shows the number of passengers and airplanes that passed through some of the world's busy airports in 1995.

Toronto Lester B. Pearson
🚶 22,353,234
✈ 342,554

Chicago O'Hare
🚶 67,253,358
✈ 900,279

Montreal Dorval
🚶 6,069,817
✈ 198,427

Seattle-Tacoma
🚶 22,790,920
✈ 386,536

Denver
🚶 31,036,622
✈ 465,903

New York J. F. Kennedy
🚶 30,379,781
✈ 340,025

Los Angeles
🚶 53,909,223
✈ 576,936

Dallas/Ft. Worth
🚶 56,490,851
✈ 879,371

Honolulu
🚶 23,672,894
✈ 373,926

Atlanta Hartsfield
🚶 57,734,755
✈ 754,108

Mexico City
🚶 15,853,812
✈ 252,347

Miami
🚶 33,235,658
✈ 576,936

San Juan Luis Muñoz Marin
🚶 9,723,800
✈ 180,269

Sao Paulo Do Guarulhos
🚶 11,939,286
✈ 140,530

KEY
🚶 passengers
✈ takeoffs and landings

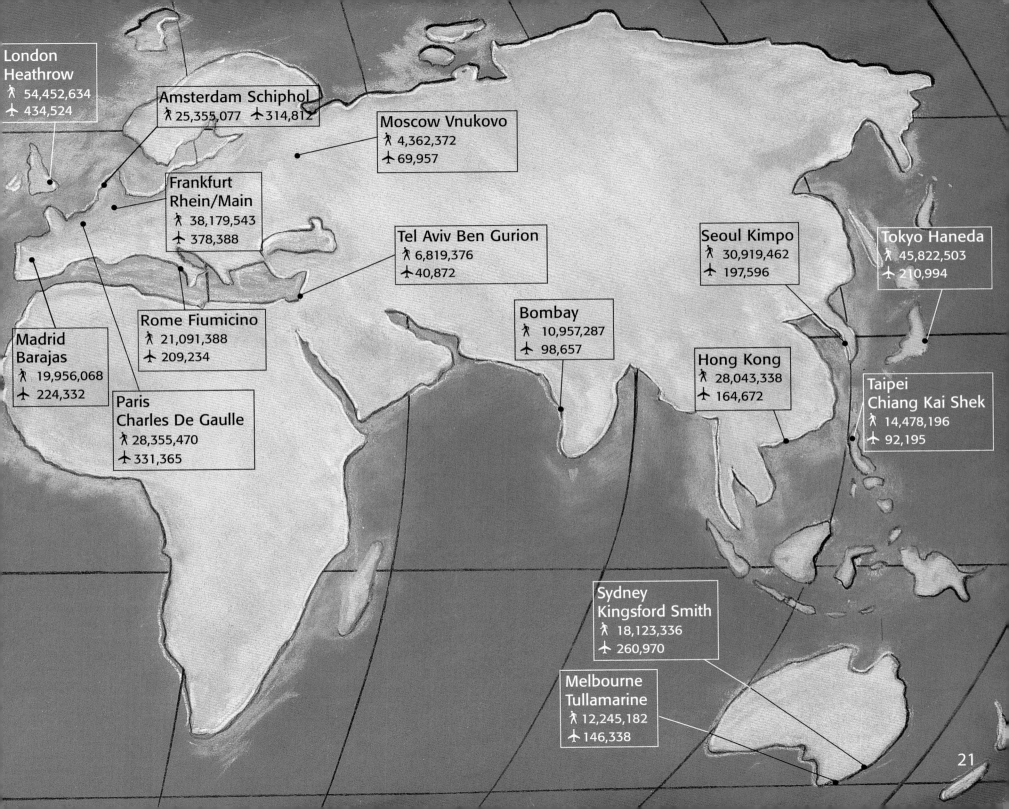

London
Heathrow
🚶 54,452,634
✈ 434,524

Amsterdam Schiphol
🚶 25,355,077   ✈ 314,812

Moscow Vnukovo
🚶 4,362,372
✈ 69,957

Frankfurt
Rhein/Main
🚶 38,179,543
✈ 378,388

Tel Aviv Ben Gurion
🚶 6,819,376
✈ 40,872

Seoul Kimpo
🚶 30,919,462
✈ 197,596

Tokyo Haneda
🚶 45,822,503
✈ 210,994

Rome Fiumicino
🚶 21,091,388
✈ 209,234

Bombay
🚶 10,957,287
✈ 98,657

Madrid
Barajas
🚶 19,956,068
✈ 224,332

Hong Kong
🚶 28,043,338
✈ 164,672

Taipei
Chiang Kai Shek
🚶 14,478,196
✈ 92,195

Paris
Charles De Gaulle
🚶 28,355,470
✈ 331,365

Sydney
Kingsford Smith
🚶 18,123,336
✈ 260,970

Melbourne
Tullamarine
🚶 12,245,182
✈ 146,338

21

GLOSSARY

airborne   in flight

airfield   landing field of an airport

altitude   height above the earth's surface

baggage   suitcases and other belongings a person takes on a trip

board   to get on a ship, a train, a bus, or an airplane

boarding pass   ticket that shows a passenger's destination, flight number, and seat number

carousel   a circular conveyor belt

catering   food service

concourse   large open area where passengers wait to board an airplane

conveyor belt   continuous belt used to carry things from one place to another

customs   where goods and baggage entering a country are checked and duty collected

de-ice   to remove ice from something, often by using chemicals

disinfectant   something used to destroy germs

dispatch office   airport office that gives a pilot flight information

duty   tax collected by customs officials for an expensive or a restricted item brought from one country to another

flap   moveable part on the wing of an airplane; used to control wind

fuel   something burned to give power or heat

gauge   instrument for measuring something

ground crew   team of people that takes care of airplanes on the ground

hangar   building in which airplanes are stored and repaired

immigration   where passports of passengers are checked

international   between or among countries

jetway   passageway between an airport terminal and an airplane that allows passengers to board and leave the plane

life jacket   safety vest used to keep a person floating in water

lift   power to begin flight

metal detector   machine used to show that metal is present

monitor   to listen or watch in order to check

nose   front tip of an airplane

oxygen mask   mask placed over the nose and mouth through which oxygen is supplied

preflight   something that happens before an airplane takes off

passport   official paper given by a government to a citizen traveling to another country

radar   instrument for determining the distance, direction, and speed of unseen objects

retract   to draw back

route   road or course that is to be traveled

runway   paved strip at an airport that an airplane uses for take off or landing

seat belt   safety strap to hold a person in a seat; used especially in cars and airplanes

subway   underground transportation system

takeoff   act of rising from the ground

taxiway   paved strip at an airport on which an airplane travels to and from a runway

terminal   main station for buses, trains, or airplanes

tug   vehicle that moves or tows other vehicles

turbulence   movements in the atmosphere that disturb wind patterns

X-ray   invisible ray that goes through solid objects and shows what is inside them

INDEX

To Judy Davis, for the invaluable gift of stories, both imagined and true,
and for teaching me how to share them—M.D.

To my three little girls, Molly, Sara, and Casey—K.D.

ACKNOWLEDGMENTS The author and publisher would like to thank Steve Klodt, Public Affairs Officer, Denver
International Airport; Andrew L. Ortiz, Airport Operations Supervisor, Denver International Airport; Bob Schulman, Vice
President of Corporate Communications, and Captain Pat Taylor, Frontier Airlines; Pilot Edward Hornung, Trans World
Airlines; Bob Leach, head of safety, and Larry Nelson, General Manager, Chelsea Catering; Mina Greenstein; and Judy Levin,
for their assistance in the preparation of this book.

Based on the book *An International Airport* by John and Yevonne Pollock

For information contact:
MONDO Publishing
980 Avenue of the Americas
New York, NY 10018
Visit our web site at http://www.mondopub.com

Designed by Mina Greenstein

Printed in China
First Mondo printing, July 1996
03 04 05 06   9 8 7 6 5 4

Library of Congress Cataloging-in-Publication Data
Davis, Meredith, 1971-
    Up and away! : taking a flight / by Meredith Davis ; illustrated by Ken Dubrowski.
       p.   cm.
    Includes index.
    Summary: Describes the varied activities involved in operating a busy airport and what happens on a passenger flight.
    ISBN 1-57255-214-X (pbk.). — ISBN 1-57255-215-8 (big book)
    1. Air travel—Juvenile literature. 2. Aeronautics, Commercial—Juvenile literature. 3. Airports—Juvenile literature.
  [1. Airports. 2. Air travel.] I. Dubrowski, Ken, ill. II. Title.
HE9787.D38   1997
910'.2'02—dc21   96-44026
                                                                                            CIP
                                                                                            AC